ENLARGED EDITION

Pictorial Guide

to

☆   ☆   ☆

COIN CONDITIONS

By Burton Hobson
and Fred Reinfeld

DOUBLEDAY & COMPANY, INC.

GARDEN CITY, NEW YORK

[1968]

ACKNOWLEDGMENTS

The authors wish to thank the many collectors and dealers whose thoughts and suggestions have been incorporated in this project and especially Mr. Harold Cohn for suggesting the idea. The enlarged condition photographs were made by the American Numismatic Society.

Revised Edition

Copyright © 1968, 1962 by
Sterling Publishing Co., Inc.
419 Park Avenue South, New York 10016

INTRODUCTION

Because of the widespread interest in coin collecting and the ever increasing number of new collectors, there has been much confusion over coin grading. An understanding of grading is essential to anyone active in the hobby. Correct grading is the basis for the proper evaluation of coins.

Coin transactions are often handled by mail and the need for condition standards in these cases is apparent. Experienced collectors are well aware that in buying, selling or trading coins there is often more dispute over grading than value.

Collectors and dealers use terms such as "Very Fine" to describe the state of preservation of their coins. Grading is the process of assigning the proper label to a given coin.

The accepted standards for each condition are given on the following pages. The decision as to whether a particular coin measures up to the set standards rests with the individual, and expressions like "slightly worn" are subject to interpretation. By photographing and enlarging actual coins representative of each condition, we are able to show pictorially the kind of coin each term indicates. The text accompanying the pictures calls attention to certain key points of each design and should be useful in differentiating between the accepted grades. The over-all condition of a coin must be taken into consideration as well as the specific points indicated.

STANDARDS FOR COIN GRADING

UNCIRCULATED (Unc.) In new condition. All lettering, the date and details of the design are extremely clear. In the modern minting process, coins slide down chutes and are packed and shipped loose in bags. Even an uncirculated coin may show a few light scratches, or abrasions, or scuff marks from this rough handling. An uncirculated coin, however, shows no sign of wear or serious damage at any point. An absolutely perfect coin is often described as Gem Uncirculated or FDC (Fleur de Coin). Uncirculated coins are often brilliant but not necessarily so.

EXTREMELY FINE (EF or XF) Similar to Uncirculated except that the very highest points of the design show the slightest signs of wear or rubbing. The first point of wear is given in the text for each different design coin. All fine detail is still clear and coins in this condition may even have a little mint luster left.

VERY FINE (VF) Design still quite clear; however, the coin begins to show definite signs of wear. The lettering may be worn but the complete outline of every letter is still clear. The highest points of the design show smooth spots of wear.

FINE (F) A considerably worn but still desirable coin. The basic outline is still clear but much of the fine detail is lost. Portions of some of the lettering may be worn away.

4

VERY GOOD (VG) A much worn but not altogether unattractive coin. A coin in this condition should be free of serious gouges or other mutilations but it may be somewhat scratched from use.

GOOD (G) A really minimum condition coin. The date and mint mark would be legible and major portions of the design distinguishable.

FAIR Coins in fair condition are usually not acceptable to collectors. They may have only partial dates, be dark in color and parts of the design may be completely worn away. They are generally used as "space fillers" only until such time as a better coin can be had.

POOR Coins in poor condition are usually highly undesirable. They may be bent, corroded and completely worn down.

Note: Proofs are coins made especially for collectors at the mint. They are struck on polished planchets from polished dies which produce coins with brilliant mirror-like surfaces, sharp edges and perfect detail. Since they are not coins made in the normal manner and are never found in circulation, they are beyond the scope of this guide. In appearance, however, they have the same perfect detail as the uncirculated coins shown plus a mirror-like surface.

HOW TO GRADE COINS

Collectors often develop their own routines for grading coins. When first starting out, however, it is a good idea to familiarize yourself with the fine detail of each type coin as shown in the photographs of the uncirculated specimens. If you know what does show on the superior pieces you will be able to tell what features of the design have been worn away on used coins of the same type.

Normal examination of the overall appearance (little or no wear, considerable wear or very much wear) will enable you to place the coin within a grade or two of its proper classification. With a 3 or 5 power glass, study the key points as shown in the pictures and outlined in the captions for the precise differentiation between the grades in question.

On the basis of the key points and the general appearance of the coin (allowance must be made for blemishes such as dents or scratches) assign the proper term to your coin.

All details of the design are extremely clear. Note especially the fine detail in the feathers and the hair, the beads in the necklace, the diamonds on the ribbon, the fullness of the facial features and the clarity of LIBERTY on the headband.

Indian Head Cent
UNCIRCULATED

The fine details of the veins in the oak leaves show in the wreath, the horizontal and vertical bars of the shield are clearly outlined, arrowheads, shafts and feathers are distinct and folds show in the ribbon.

7

The very highest points show slight signs of wear. Spots of wear appear on the hair above the ear, the fourth bead of the necklace, the second diamond on the ribbon and the tips of the feathers.

Indian Head Cent
EXTREMELY FINE

Spots of wear appear on the ribbon where it wraps around the arrows and in the fine horizontal lines of the shield.

Design still clear but definite signs of wear begin to show. Fine lines in the feathers are gone, the middle beads and diamonds are smooth. LIBERTY is worn but the outline of each individual letter is still clear.

Indian Head Cent
VERY FINE

Portions of the leaves in the shield show smooth spots. The vertical lines of the shield are clear but the horizontal lines are no longer sharp.

Considerable signs of wear are apparent. Portions of the letters in LIBERTY are worn away but most of the letters are still visible. The diamonds are completely gone and only the end beads of the necklace are clear. Only the heaviest lines remain in the feathers.

Indian Head Cent
FINE

The knot of the ribbon is smooth. The feathers on the arrows show wear. The vertical bars of the shield are no longer sharp.

The outline of the head, letters and date are clear but much worn. LIBERTY is gone, no beads show and no detail is visible in the feathers. The top outline of the headband still shows.

Indian Head Cent
VERY GOOD

Only coarse detail of the leaves remains. All fine lines in the shield are worn smooth and the shafts of the arrows are partly worn away.

11

A very flat coin. All fullness is gone from the mouth, nose and chin. The denticles around the edge of the coin are worn smooth.

Indian Head Cent
GOOD

The wreath is visible only in outline. The horizontal lines in the shield are completely gone. The denticles around the edge of the coin are worn smooth.

The details of Lincoln's hair, beard and features are sharp and clear. The lines of his coat, shirt and tie are distinct.

Lincoln Head Cent
UNCIRCULATED

The grains and parallel lines of the wheat stalk stand out sharply on the reverse.

13

The cheek and jaw bone are the highest points of the obverse design and show the first traces of wear.

Lincoln Head Cent
EXTREMELY FINE

The lines of the wheat stalk are clear and distinct. There is slight wear on the inside row of grains.

Definite wear shows in the hair around the ear. There is a smooth spot at the top of the ear.

Lincoln Head Cent
VERY FINE

The lines of the stalk are plain but slightly smooth, and the grains of wheat near the top of the stalk are less distinct.

The ear shows considerable wear. The back and bottom edges are less distinct. The cheek and jawbone are fairly worn.

Lincoln Head Cent
FINE

The parallel lines of the stalk have smooth areas, particularly near the top of the left stalk. Each grain is visible but no longer sharply defined.

All fine detail is gone from the hair and beard. Only a rough outline of the ear is visible. The left end of the bowtie is only vague.

Lincoln Head Cent
VERY GOOD

Only portions of the parallel lines still show. The remaining portions are very faded.

A very much worn coin. The hairline is indistinct. The area between the cheek and jaw bone is completely smooth and only a trace of an opening marks what remains of the ear.

Lincoln Head Cent
GOOD

The lines of the wheat stalks are worn smooth. Only the vaguest outline of the grains can be seen.

Only the outline of Lincoln's head is visible. The outline even of the shirt and coat collar are worn smooth.

Lincoln Head Cent
FAIR

The stalks are completely smooth. The rim of the coin is quite flat.

A coin in poor condition can be recognized as to date and mint but beyond that it may be pitted, corroded, dark or even bent. These minimum condition coins are generally unattractive.

Lincoln Head Cent
POOR

The rim is worn down even into the tops of the letters. A coin in poor condition is not worth collecting except possibly as a space filler for the rare dates.

The design perfectly clear.
Much fine detail is apparent in the hair, coronet and spray of leaves. The majority of the stars show points depending upon how sharply struck the coin is.

Liberty Head Nickel
UNCIRCULATED

Much detail appears in the wreath, particularly in the corn ears and wheat grain.

21

Slight signs of wear on the very highest points; the forehead just above the eyebrow, the waves of hair below B of LIBERTY and the top blossom in the spray of leaves.

Liberty Head Nickel
EXTREMELY FINE

Spots of wear show on the left and right top leaves of the wreath.

Design sharp but definite signs of wear begin to show. Smooth areas appear in the hair above the ear and in the chignon (bun) at back of the head. All letters in LIBERTY visible and strong except possibly the I which must at least show.

Liberty Head Nickel
VERY FINE

The kernels of corn at the bottom and the grains of wheat at the top are partially worn away.

Much detail of the hair is gone showing considerable sign of wear. The small curl at the nape of the neck is gone and the hairline above the temple is smooth. LIBERTY is readable although the I may be faint.

Liberty Head Nickel
FINE

The detail of the lower leaves is gone and the heads of wheat are smooth.

A much worn coin. All details of the hair are gone. The cheek and jawline are smooth. LIBERTY will not show more than parts of two or three letters.

Liberty Head Nickel
VERY GOOD

The wreath is visible only in outline. All lettering is visible but faint. The knot of the ribbon bow is quite flat.

A really minimum condition, smooth coin. The date is readable but all fullness of the design is gone. The head shows up in outline only. Denticles at the edge of the coin are worn down.

Liberty Head Nickel
GOOD

Parts of some letters may be worn away or be very faint. The rim of the coin is worn flat.

The Indian's head does not have the same fine detail as designs of many other U.S. coins. Cheekbone is full, the date, feathers and braid are sharp.

Buffalo Nickel
UNCIRCULATED

The buffalo has a full, rounded horn and the tip of the tail shows distinctly. The blanket of hair on the shoulder is clearly defined.

A slight spot of wear shows on the highest point, the ribbon on the braid of hair.

Buffalo Nickel
EXTREMELY FINE

The tip of the tail and the shoulder hair show slight wear.

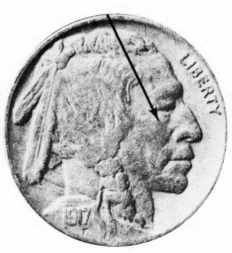

Definite signs of wear appear on the Indian's cheekbone and in the hair above the ribbon. The date is clear and sharp but worn down a little.

Buffalo Nickel
VERY FINE

The top of the horn is faded but distinct; much of the roundness is lost. The fine detail is gone from the shoulder hair.

The Indian's hair is considerably worn and the tops of the feathers are smooth. The date is faded but each digit is still legible.

Buffalo Nickel
FINE

The top of the horn is no longer distinguishable and the tip of the tail is completely worn away. The outline of the shoulder hair above the front leg is gone.

A coin in this condition shows much wear and all fine detail is lost. The rim may be worn down into the top of the letters in LIBERTY. The date must, of course, be identifiable although portions may not be clearly defined.

Buffalo Nickel
VERY GOOD

Only the base of the horn remains. The shoulder and rear leg are worn smooth. The rim may be worn down into the edge of the lettering.

This series is usually collected in uncirculated condition only. Specimens in less than EF condition are still considered pocket change with the exception of one or two scarce dates.

Jefferson Nickel
UNCIRCULATED

Recent dates, particularly from the Philadelphia mint, have been poorly struck, have little detail on the reverse and are often scratched.

Wear first appears on Jefferson's eyebrow, cheekbone and the lower back part of his hair.

Jefferson Nickel
EXTREMELY FINE

The first signs of wear show on the steps and on the outline of the lintel above the doorway.

The outline of the ribbon and the letters in LIBERTY are sharp. The leaves in the laurel wreath are clearly defined. There is a roundness to the cheek and features of the face.

Liberty Head Dime
UNCIRCULATED

Much fine detail stands out in the heads of wheat and the ear of corn.

Traces of wear show on the cheek and on the lock of hair just above the eye.

Liberty Head Dime
EXTREMELY FINE

Slight signs of wear appear on the grains of wheat at the top of the wreath and on the bow of the ribbon.

35

LIBERTY on the head-band is clear but the bottom outline of the ribbon is faint. Curl in front of ear shows unmistakable signs of wear.

Liberty Head Dime
VERY FINE

Definite wear shows on the large leaf at the left of the wreath and on the kernels of the ear of corn at right.

Only partial LIBERTY is clear, TY especially being faint. The top outline of the ribbon and the outline of the laurel wreath are weak. The cheek has a decidedly flat appearance.

Liberty Head Dime
FINE

A considerable amount of wear is apparent on the cluster of oak leaves and the rest of the wreath. The knot of the ribbon is flat.

A much worn coin. LIBERTY is completely worn away except for a letter or two. The bottom of the laurel wreath, the curl in front of the ear and the eyebrow are all worn smooth.

Liberty Head Dime
VERY GOOD

Only the outline and coarse detail remain of the wreath.

A very worn coin. The head is seen only in outline, the rim is flat.

Liberty Head Dime
GOOD

The wreath is visible only in outline.

Very clear detail on wings, helmet and hair above forehead and in front of ear.

Mercury Head Dime
UNCIRCULATED

Vertical rods in the fasces bundle are sharply outlined. Diagonal and horizontal bands stand out clearly.

The hair above the fore-head and in front of the ear show slight signs of wear. A spot of wear shows on the front of the wing.

Mercury Head Dime
EXTREMELY FINE

The diagonal bands show traces of wear but the horizontal bands are clear.

Much of the detail is gone from the braid of hair across the front of the head. There is definite wear on the cap and wing.

Mercury Head Dime
VERY FINE

The vertical rods in the bundle have lost some of their clarity but are still visible. The horizontal bands show spots of wear.

The fine detail of the cap, hair and wing is worn away. The hairline is no longer distinct.

Mercury Head Dime
FINE

The diagonal and horizontal bands are visible only at their ends. The centermost of the vertical rods are smooth.

The hair, cap and wing are smooth. Only the coarse outline of the feathers remains.

Mercury Head Dime
VERY GOOD

The vertical rods and the horizontal and diagonal bands are nearly smooth. The rim of the coin is flat.

This series is generally collected in uncirculated condition since all of the issues are still recent enough to be readily available. The finest detail is in the hairlines and the hair just above the ear is the first point to show wear.

Roosevelt Dime
UNCIRCULATED

The flame and the lines of the torch are sharply defined. Wear will appear first on the lines of the flame.

Liberty Head Quarter
UNCIRCULATED

Liberty's cap and hair, the laurel wreath and the LIBERTY
ribbon are well defined.

Liberty Head Quarter
UNCIRCULATED

The reverse shows more fine detail than most U.S. coins. The feathers, shield, ribbon and arrows are sharply outlined.

Liberty Head Quarter
EXTREMELY FINE

Slight signs of wear show on the hair above the eye and on the top fold of the cap.

Liberty Head Quarter
EXTREMELY FINE

Traces of wear show on the eagle's head, wing tips and the center tail feather.

Liberty Head Quarter
VERY FINE

Definite areas of wear show on the forelock, cheek and laurel wreath. LIBERTY is clear but the bottom outline of the ribbon is weak.

Liberty Head Quarter
VERY FINE

There is unmistakable wear on the eagle's head, wings and tail. The claw grasping the arrows is smooth. The vertical lines of the shield are weak.

Liberty Head Quarter
FINE

Only partial LIBERTY is clear, RTY especially being faint. The top outline of the ribbon and the outline of the laurel wreath are vague.

Liberty Head Quarter
FINE

Considerable wear is apparent on the reverse. UNUM is faded on the ribbon. The horizontal lines of the shield are weak. The feathers on the eagle's legs are smooth.

Liberty Head Quarter
VERY GOOD

LIBERTY is completely worn away except for a letter or two. Only a coarse outline of the laurel wreath remains.

Liberty Head Quarter
VERY GOOD

The reverse shows much wear. The lines of the shield are smooth, portions of the legend are no longer visible on the ribbon, and only the coarsest outline of the feathers remains.

Liberty Head Quarter
GOOD

The head shows only in outline. No part of LIBERTY is visible. The rim is worn flat.

Liberty Head Quarter
GOOD

The eagle is visible only in outline. The eye is no longer distinct. The rim is worn flat.

Standing Liberty Quarter
UNCIRCULATED

Fine detail stands out on Liberty's chain mail shirt. The folds of her drapery and sash are distinct. The head often has a flat appearance even on uncirculated coins and, therefore, is not a significant grading factor. Specimens with rounded, full heads are especially desirable.

Standing Liberty Quarter
UNCIRCULATED

The feathers on the eagle's wings, neck and body are sharply outlined.

Standing Liberty Quarter
EXTREMELY FINE

Traces of wear show on the right leg, particularly at the knee and on the sash across her body.

Standing Liberty Quarter
EXTREMELY FINE

Slight wear shows on the eagle's breast.

Standing Liberty Quarter
VERY FINE

Definite wear shows on the chain mail across Liberty's
breast. The fold of drapery across the right leg is smooth.

Standing Liberty Quarter
VERY FINE

Worn areas are apparent along the front of the eagle's wing and its neck.

Standing Liberty Quarter
FINE

There is considerable wear on both breasts but some detail of the armor, particularly on the shoulders, remains. The toes on the foot are no longer distinct.

Standing Liberty Quarter
FINE

Most of the fine detail of the feathers at the tip of the
wing is lost.

Standing Liberty Quarter
VERY GOOD

The body and the leg of Liberty are now quite flat. The device on the shield is vague. Wear may extend into the date but each digit must be discernible.

Standing Liberty Quarter
VERY GOOD

Only the coarse outline of the feathers shows on the wing.

Washington Quarter
UNCIRCULATED

These coins are ordinarily collected in uncirculated or extremely fine condition although there are a few dates that are becoming difficult to locate in choice condition. Much fine detail is apparent in the hair.

Washington Quarter
UNCIRCULATED

The eagle's feathers are clearly defined on its breast, wings and legs.

Washington Quarter
EXTREMELY FINE

The first traces of wear on this design appear on the hair just back of the ear.

Washington Quarter
EXTREMELY FINE

The first spots of wear show on the eagle's breast and the tops of the legs.

Liberty Head Half
UNCIRCULATED

Liberty's cap and hair, the laurel wreath and the ribbon on
which LIBERTY is placed are sharply defined.

Liberty Head Half
UNCIRCULATED

The reverse of this design carries finer detail than most
other U.S. coins. The feathers, shield, ribbon and arrows
are clearly outlined.

Liberty Head Half
EXTREMELY FINE

Slight signs of wear show on the forelock of hair just above
Liberty's brow and on the top fold of her cap.

Liberty Head Half
EXTREMELY FINE

The eagle's head, wing tips and the center tail feather show
slight wear.

Liberty Head Half
VERY FINE

Wear shows in spots on the forelock, cheek and laurel wreath. LIBERTY is clear but the bottom outline of the ribbon is weak.

Liberty Head Half
VERY FINE

There are definite areas of wear on the eagle's head, wings and tail. The claw grasping the arrows is smooth. The lines of the shield are faded.

Liberty Head Half
FINE

LIBERTY is only partially clear, the last letters being particularly faint. The top outline of the ribbon and the outline of the laurel wreath are not distinct.

Liberty Head Half
FINE

The reverse shows considerable wear. UNUM is faded on the ribbon, the lines in the shield are only partially visible, and the feathers on the eagle's legs are smooth.

Liberty Head Half
VERY GOOD

LIBERTY is completely worn away except possibly for portions of a few letters. Only a coarse outline of the laurel wreath remains.

Liberty Head Half
VERY GOOD

Much wear is apparent on the reverse. Portions of the
legend are no longer visible on the ribbon and only the
rough outline of the shield remains.

Walking Liberty Half Dollar
UNCIRCULATED

The folds and lines of Liberty's drapery are clear. The
head, body and arm are rounded. The stars stand out
sharply on the flag.

Walking Liberty Half Dollar
UNCIRCULATED

The feathers on the eagle's body, wings and legs are sharply outlined.

Walking Liberty Half Dollar
EXTREMELY FINE

Traces of wear show on Liberty's cap and down the length
of her left leg.

Walking Liberty Half Dollar
EXTREMELY FINE

Slight wear shows on the highest part of the eagle's breast and the front edge of the closest leg.

Walking Liberty Half Dollar
VERY FINE

Wear is apparent across the breast and on the flowers in
Liberty's arm. The lines in her drapery are faded.

Walking Liberty Half Dollar
VERY FINE

There is a definite area of wear on the eagle's breast and on the tip of the wing.

Walking Liberty Half Dollar
FINE

There is a smooth line of wear down Liberty's side from the shoulder to the ankle. Worn spots show on the sandal and the fold of the flag.

Walking Liberty Half Dollar
FINE

Considerable wear is apparent down the side of the eagle's
body and leg and along the front edge of the wing. The
feathers on the eagle's right leg show a spot of wear.

Walking Liberty Half Dollar
VERY GOOD

A much worn coin in this condition. Liberty is visible only in outline. Wear shows also in the field of the flag.

Walking Liberty Half Dollar
VERY GOOD

All fine detail is gone from the eagle's body. The claws grasping the branch are no longer distinct.

Franklin Half Dollar
UNCIRCULATED

The detail of the portrait is weak even on uncirculated specimens. The first traces of wear appear on the hair above and
back of the ear and on the curl on the ends of the strands.

Franklin Half Dollar
UNCIRCULATED

The writing on the bell is vague even on uncirculated specimens. Wear first shows on the high part of the horizontal lines at the top of the bell and on the horizontal lines at the bottom just above the clapper.

Kennedy Half Dollar
UNCIRCULATED

This newest type U.S. coin is usually collected in uncirculated condition since all of the issues are still recent enough to be readily available. The points of highest wear are on the hair just above the ear and on the jawbone.

Kennedy Half Dollar
UNCIRCULATED

The first traces of wear appear on the wings at the point where the first feather joins the edge of the wing. Wear starts to show soon after on the head of the eagle.

Liberty Head Silver Dollar
UNCIRCULATED

There is a great amount of detail visible in Liberty's hair. Fine detail shows in the spray of flowers and leaves and in the folds of her cap.

Liberty Head Silver Dollar
UNCIRCULATED

The feathers of the eagle's breast, head, legs, tail and wings are clear and sharply defined.

Liberty Head Silver Dollar
EXTREMELY FINE

The first slight signs of wear appear in the hair above the forehead.

Liberty Head Silver Dollar
EXTREMELY FINE

Traces of wear show on the highest part of the eagle's breast.

Liberty Head Silver Dollar
VERY FINE

Definite wear is visible in the hair above the ear and on the spray of flowers and leaves.

Liberty Head Silver Dollar
VERY FINE

Wear is apparent on the eagle's head and the tips of its wings.

Liberty Head Silver Dollar
FINE

Considerable wear shows in the hair. There are smooth
spots in the hair below the ear and at the back of the neck.

Liberty Head Silver Dollar
FINE

The eagle's legs and tail feathers have worn spots. The breast and head are worn quite smooth.

Liberty Head Silver Dollar
VERY GOOD

All fine detail is lacking in the hair. The spray of flowers and leaves and the folds of the cap are smooth. The curl of hair in front of the ear is no longer distinct.

Liberty Head Silver Dollar
VERY GOOD

Only the rough outline of the wing feathers remains. No
fine detail appears on the eagle's body. The cross point of
the arrow shafts and the olive branch is no longer distinct.

Peace Dollar
UNCIRCULATED

These coins are ordinarily collected in uncirculated or extremely fine condition. The series was struck from rather shallow dies and even uncirculated coins do not exhibit the sharp detail seen on many other U.S. coins. The strands of hair are clearly defined.

Peace Dollar
UNCIRCULATED

Clear outlines of the feathers show on the eagle's head,
wings, legs and tail. The lettering is weak even on uncirculated coins.

Peace Dollar
EXTREMELY FINE

The first sign of wear shows on the lock of hair crossing
over the band of the coronet and in the hair above Liberty's
ear.

Peace Dollar
EXTREMELY FINE

Traces of wear show at the top and along the front edge
of the eagle's closest wing.

POINTS OF HIGHEST WEAR

On each different coin design there are certain key points to inspect in order to assign a condition grade to any given specimen. The most important parts of a coin design, so far as the process of grading is concerned, are the points of highest wear. Every coin has certain features of the design that stand out from the remainder of the coin and these are the first areas to bump or rub against other coins or objects. The absence or presence of wear on these high points determine whether a coin is uncirculated or used. The relative amount of wear on a used coin determines its exact grade as shown on the preceding pages in the enlarged photograph of various coins over a range of conditions for the same type. In this section you will find photographs of superior condition specimens of earlier issue U.S. silver and base-metal coins and all issues of U.S. gold. Arrows on the photographs accurately point out the important details —the points of highest wear.

HALF CENTS

Liberty Head with Cap on Pole

The points of highest wear for both obverse types are on the hair above the forehead and the ridge of the shoulder. On the reverse, wear first shows on the knot of the bow. Coins of this type are seldom well struck on both obverse and reverse.

Draped Bust of Liberty

The hair above the forehead and over the ear and the folds of the drapery show signs of wear after very little circulation. The points to check on the reverse are the leaves of the olive branches and the knot of the ribbon.

Turban Head of Liberty

Wear first appears on the hair above and below the head band. The B of LIBERTY is a high point of the design, the other letters showing wear also in the lesser condition grades. Traces of wear on the reverse appear first on the leaves of the laurel wreath and the knot of the ribbon.

Liberty Head with Coronet

Coins of this type were well struck in deep relief and considerable detail remains even on specimens in the lower grades of condition. Wear does show quickly on the hair behind the ear and on the curls above and below the truncation of the bust. On the reverse, the leaves and the knot first show wear.

Liberty Head with Flowing Hair

The points of first wear on this type are the high ridges of hair. The intersections of the links of chain itself are the key feature of the chain type reverse and on the wreath type reverse, the knot and bow of the bow are the points to check. Many coins of this series were weak strikes and may not show sharp detail even though they do not show sign of much actual wear.

Liberty Head with Cap on Pole

Wear first shows on the lock of hair above the forehead and on the highest point of the shoulder. On the reverse, the leaves of the wreath and the knot and bow of the ribbon are the first areas to be worn down.

Draped Bust of Liberty

The high point of the hair above the forehead is again the first spot to show wear followed by the curl of hair above the ear. The folds of the drapery also show wear quickly. The bow and knot of the ribbon and the leaves of the olive branches are the key features of the reverse.

Turban Head of Liberty.
The first trace of wear on this type
appears on the curl of hair just
above the eye. The leaves of the
laurel wreath and the ribbon are
the points to check on the reverse.

Liberty Head with Coronet.
Coins of this type were well struck
in deep relief and considerable
details remain even on specimens
in the lower grades of condition.
The first signs of wear are found
on the locks of hair above the eye
and above the ear. The highest
points of the reverse are the leaves
of the wreath and the ribbon.

FLYING EAGLE CENT

The feathers of the eagle on this type are sharp and well defined and the
amount of wear they show determines the state of preservation of any
given coin. The highest points of the design are the breast, thigh and the
tip of the right wing. The highest point of the reverse design is the knot
of the ribbon.

113

TWO CENTS

The key feature in determining the condition of this coin is the WE of the motto IN GOD WE TRUST and that is where the first signs of wear appear. On the reverse, wear shows first on the ribbon and the grains of wheat.

THREE CENTS (SILVER)

Because of the small size and thinness of these coins, many were weakly struck and some unworn specimens lack detail. The points of highest wear are the fine raised lines running in toward the center of the coin from each point of the star. The highest point of the reverse is the middle digit of the Roman numeral III.

THREE CENTS (NICKEL)

Due to the hardness of the metal and the mint's lack of experience with nickel, many of these coins were weakly struck. Wear does first appear on the wave of hair above the ear and on the reverse on the vertical lines of the Roman numeral.

114

HALF DIMES

Liberty Head with Flowing Hair

The point of highest wear for this type is the lock of hair above the forehead. On the reverse, wear shows first on the eagle's breast.

Draped Bust of Liberty

The wave of hair above the forehead and the folds of drapery at the shoulder and bust are the spots that first show wear on this design. On the small eagle reverse, the key point is the eagle's breast. On the large heraldic eagle reverse, the eagle's head and tail feathers and the ribbon are the highest features of the design.

Liberty Head Wearing Cap

Wear shows first on the lock of hair above the eye and the fold of drapery at the front of the bust. The eagle's head, wing tips and claws are the points to check on the reverse.

Seated Figure of Liberty

On this design the areas of greatest wear are the folds of drapery over the right shoulder and at the knee. The leaves of the wreath are the first points of wear on the reverse.

SHIELD NICKEL

On many uncirculated coins of this type, the fine horizontal lines of the shield are weak. The highest point of the design however is on the small cross above the shield, followed by the tips of the olive leaves. Wear first appears on the reverse at the back part of the curve of the numeral 5.

DIMES

Draped Bust of Liberty
The points of highest wear are the wave of hair above the forehead and the folds of drapery at the shoulder and bust. On the reverse, wear shows first on the breast of the small eagle and on the head and tail feathers of the large heraldic eagle. The high points of the ribbon are also very susceptible to wear.

Liberty Head Wearing Cap
Traces of wear show first on the lock of hair above the eye and on the fold of drapery at the front of the bust. On the reverse, the key features are the eagle's head, claws and wing tips.

Seated Figure of Liberty
Wear shows first on the folds of drapery over the right shoulder and at the knee. On the reverse, which has different wreaths depending upon the date, the highest points are the leaves.

TWENTY CENTS

The points of highest wear are the head, arm and knee. In the lesser grades of condition, the letters of the word LIBERTY become worn, beginning with the LI. On this design the eagle's feathers are sharp and well-defined. Wear shows first on the center of the breast.

Draped Bust of Liberty

Like the other denominations of this type, the points of highest wear are the wave of hair above the forehead and the folds of drapery at the shoulder and bust. The breast of the small eagle is the key spot for that reverse and the head, tail feathers and ribbon all show wear quickly on the large, heraldic eagle reverse.

Liberty Head Wearing Cap

Traces of wear appear first on the hair above the forehead and on the top of the cap. On the reverse, the features to check are the eagle's claws.

Seated Figure of Liberty

The arm and knees are the first features of this design to show signs of wear. On the reverse, the key points are the eagle's head and the top of his wings.

117

HALF DOLLARS

Liberty Head with Flowing Hair
The point of highest wear on this type is the wave of hair just above the forehead. On the reverse it is the eagle's breast.

Draped Bust of Liberty
Wear reveals itself first on the curl of hair above the forehead and on the folds of drapery at the shoulder and the bust. On the small eagle reverse, the eagle's breast is the highest point of the design and, on the large, heraldic eagle reverse, the eagle's head, tail feathers and wing tips are the key spots. The high points of the ribbon in the eagle's beak also show spots of wear quickly.

Liberty Head Wearing Cap

Traces of wear show first on the lock of hair above the forehead and then on the top of the cap and the drapery clasp at the shoulders. The eagle's claws and the arrowheads are the first features of the reverse design to show wear, followed by the eagle's neck and wing tips.

Seated Figure of Liberty

As on coins of other denominations with this design, the areas that show wear first are the head and knees. The drapery clasp at the shoulder and Liberty's arm are also susceptible to wear. The key features on the reverse are the eagle's neck and the tops of the wings.

Liberty Head with Flowing Hair

As on the lower denomination coins of this design, wear appears quickly on the wave of hair above the forehead. On the silver dollar the eyebrow line is also a point of highest wear. The areas to check on the reverse are the eagle's breast and left leg.

Draped Bust of Liberty

The points of highest wear are the waves of hair above the forehead and behind the eye, followed by the folds of drapery at the shoulder and bust. On the small eagle reverse the eagle's breast and left leg are most susceptible to wear. On the large heraldic eagle, the key features are the eagle's head and tail feathers and the high points of the ribbon on which the motto is inscribed.

Seated Figure of Liberty

The knees and breast are the first features to show traces of wear on this type. The head and cap also wear quickly. The highest points of the reverse design are the eagle's head and the tops of the wings and the top point of the shield on his breast.

TRADE DOLLAR

For this design, the points of highest wear are the hair just below the coronet, the shoulder and the knees. Another area to check is the top of the bundle of wheat behind the figure of Liberty. Wear on the reverse appears first on the eagle's head and the top of the left wing.

GOLD DOLLARS

Liberty Head with Coronet
The point of highest wear for this type is the hair below the coronet and behind the ear. On the reverse, the leaves of the laurel wreath are the first features to show wear.

Liberty Head with Feathered Crown
The first traces of wear on this type show on the curled tips of the feathers of the crown. The corn, wheat, tobacco and cotton of the wreath are the points to check on the reverse.

QUARTER EAGLES ($2½)

Liberty Head with Peaked Cap
The top of the cap, the hair above the forehead and the drapery at the neckline are the first points of the design to show the effects of circulation. The eagle's wing tips and head and the clouds and scroll are the features of the reverse most susceptible to wear.

Turban Head of Liberty
Wear shows first on the folds of the cap and the hair above the forehead. The features worn quickly on the reverse are the eagle's head and neck. The 1808 date (a rare type) also has a fold of drapery that is a point of high wear.

Liberty Head with Coronet
Wear on this type can be detected first at the point of the coronet, on the hair just above it and on the curl over the ear. The reverse quickly shows wear on the eagle's neck and wing tips.

Indian Head
The entire design is sunk into the planchet of this coin. The highest point of the obverse is the Indian's cheekbone and that of the reverse the feathers on the upper part of the eagle's wing.

122

THREE DOLLAR GOLD

The points of greatest wear for this type are the curled tips of the feathers of the crown, the wave of hair above the forehead and, on the reverse, the highest features of the wreath.

HALF EAGLES ($5)

Liberty Head with Peaked Cap
The three key points of this type are the top of the cap, the curl of hair above the forehead and the drapery of the bust. The eagle's breast is the point of highest wear on the reverse.

Turban Head of Liberty
The first features to show wear are the folds of the cap, the hair above the forehead and the fold of drapery at the bust. The eagle's head and neck are the features of the reverse that wear most quickly.

Liberty Head with Coronet
Traces of wear appear first at the point of the coronet, on the wave of hair above it and on the curl over the ear. The eagle's neck and wing tips are the first areas to wear on the reverse.

Indian Head
The highest point of the design is the Indian's cheekbone. On the reverse, the area of feathers on the upper part of the eagle's wing is the key feature in judging condition.

Liberty Head with Peaked Cap

The points of highest wear for this type are the folds of the cap, the hair behind the ear and the drapery at the neckline. On the small eagle reverse, the breast is the key point; on the large heraldic eagle reverse, it is the wing tips.

Liberty Head with Coronet

The first areas to show wear on this design are the upper edge of the coronet, the waves of hair above it and the curl of hair over the ear. The eagle's neck and wing tips are the first points on the reverse to show the effects of circulation.

Liberty with Feather Headdress

On this design the first traces of wear appear on the waves of hair above the forehead and the ear. On the reverse, the finely detailed feathers of the eagle's wing show wear after very little handling.

DOUBLE EAGLES ($20)

Liberty Head with Coronet
The hair above the forehead, the waves of hair at the top of the head and the curl above the ear are the points of highest wear. On the reverse, the tips of the wings are the highest points. These large, heavy coins even in un-circulated conditions nearly always have some small circles and scratches called "bag marks."

Standing Liberty
The first spots of wear on this type appear on the forehead, nose and right knee. Traces of wear also appear quickly on the breast. The finely detailed eagle on the reverse shows wear quickly on the breast and on the top edge of the left wing.

CANADA
GREAT BRITAIN

Canadian Large Cent
UNCIRCULATED

Much fine detail appears on the crown and in the hair, uniform and decorations. Large cents were also issued during the reigns of Queen Victoria and King Edward VII and the standards for grading them are similar to the coins of King George V.

Canadian Large Cent
UNCIRCULATED

The garland of leaves and
the circle of dots stand out
in sharp relief.

Canadian Large Cent
EXTREMELY FINE

Traces of wear show on the center circle of the patteé cross at the side of the crown, at the tip of the moustache and on the ribbon at the shoulder.

Canadian Large Cent
EXTREMELY FINE

The high rim of this issue protects the reverse design and the only sign of wear on a slightly used coin is a slightly flat rim.

Canadian Large Cent
VERY FINE

The center circle of the patteé cross at the side of the crown is worn smooth. The diamond on the headband above the ear is faint. The decorations across the chest are worn.

Canadian Large Cent
VERY FINE

Signs of wear show on the high edges of the leaves in the garland around the edge of the coin.

Canadian Large Cent
FINE

The horizontal lines of the headband are worn smooth at the center. The ribbon on the shoulder is vague.

Canadian Large Cent
FINE

Definite wear is apparent on the garland of leaves. The tips and all edges of the leaves are smooth.

Canadian Large Cent
VERY GOOD

All fine detail of the crown, hair and uniform is worn away. The decoration at the throat is not distinct.

Canadian Large Cent
VERY GOOD

The fine detail of the leaves is no longer visible. The circle of dots is flat. Some of the lettering is faint.

Fine detail shows on the crown, hair, uniform and decorations. Small cents were also issued during the reign of King George VI and are being struck annually under Queen Elizabeth. The standards for the later issues are the same as for the coins of George V.

Canadian Small Cent
UNCIRCULATED

The veins and petioles of the maple leaves stand out clearly.

The first signs of wear appear on the diamond on the headband of the crown and on the tip of the moustache.

Canadian Small Cent
EXTREMELY FINE

The reverse is protected by the high rim on this series and the only sign of wear on the reverse of a slightly used coin is a flatter rim.

The detail of the headband is faint. The point of the moustache is not distinct.

Canadian Small Cent
VERY FINE

There are smooth spots of wear at the tips of the maple leaves.

The decorations across the chest are worn smooth. The horizontal lines on the headband of the crown are not distinct.

Canadian Small Cent
FINE

Wear extends into the center of each leaf.

The fine detail of the crown, hair, uniform and decorations are no longer visible.

Canadian Small Cent
VERY GOOD

The veins of the leaves are worn smooth and only the petioles remain.

The crown, hair, uniform and decorations show much fine detail. Five cent pieces of this size were also issued during the reign of King George VI and are being struck annually under Queen Elizabeth (12-sided since 1942). The condition standards for the later issues are the same as for the coins of King George V.

Canadian Large Five Cents
UNCIRCULATED

The veins and petioles of the maple leaves stand out distinctly.

The first traces of wear appear on the patteé cross at the side of the crown and at the tip of the moustache.

Canadian Large Five Cents
EXTREMELY FINE

The reverse of this design is protected by the high rim, and the only sign of wear on a slightly used coin is a somewhat flatter rim.

The detail of the headband on the crown is faint. The patteé cross at the side of the crown and the tip of the moustache are not distinct.

Canadian Large Five Cents
VERY FINE

There are smooth spots of wear at the tips of the maple leaves.

The details of the decorations across the chest are worn quite smooth. The horizontal lines of the headband of the crown are not distinct.

Canadian Large Five Cents
FINE

Areas of wear extend into the center of the leaves.

The detail of the crown, hair, uniform and decorations is no longer visible.

Canadian Large Five Cents
VERY GOOD

The veins of the leaves are worn away and only the petioles can be seen.

British Penny
FLEUR DE COIN
(UNCIRCULATED)

Many fine details are apparent on the tiara, necklace and the decoration attached to the gown. The folds of the veil and the hair line are sharply designed.

British Penny
FLEUR DE COIN
(UNCIRCULATED)

Britannia's helmet, gown and shield are sharply defined. This design type has been continued through the following reigns.

British Penny
EXTREMELY FINE

The first traces of wear appear on the cheekbone and eyebr6w line and on the edge of the veil at its high point near the decoration.

British Penny
EXTREMELY FINE

The points of highest wear for this design are the knee and the
visor of the helmet which show slight signs of wear in this
condition.

British Penny
VERY FINE

In this grade wear is more pronounced on the highest points and appears also on some of the fine detail—the patteé cross at the top of the tiara, the medallion of the necklace and the decoration.

British Penny
VERY FINE

Additional spots of wear show on the shoulder, breast, arm and hands. The fairly high rim on this coin protects the design well enough so that much detail remains on coins that have not been extensively circulated.

British Penny
FINE

Considerable wear is apparent on specimens in this condition. The fine detail of the tiara and necklace are faded. The hair line is no longer distinct.

British Penny
FINE

Wear is apparent also on the reverse design, the whole of the arm and leg being smoothed out. The fingers of the hand grasping the trident are no longer individually discernible.

British Penny
GOOD

Only the general outline of the design remains. The side of
the face and the veil are worn flat. The decoration is worn
away completely.

British Penny
GOOD

The reverse also shows much wear. The detail of the foot and helmet are gone. Even the emblem on the shield is partly faded away.

British Penny
POOR

A coin in poor condition can be recognized as to type and date but beyond that may be pitted, corroded, dark and generally unattractive.

British Penny
POOR

The rim is worn down to the point where some of the letters
are no longer visible. These minimum condition coins are not
worth collecting except as space fillers for rare dates or types.

INDEX